Yo, Ho, Ho! Write a Pirate's Adventure

Search for Buried Treasure!

By Jan May

Yo, Ho, Ho! Write a Pirate's Adventure

Copyright 2021 by Jan May

Education and Language Arts

First Edition

ISBN 978-1-7321119-2-9

All rights reserved. No portion of this book may be copied, shared, given away or reproduced in any manner, whatsoever.

Printed in the United States of America

Published by New Millennium Girl Books

Clip Art by Kate Hadfield Designs https://katehadfielddesigns.com/
Artifex https://www.teacherspayteachers.com/Store/Artifex

Contents

Introduction - Teacher's Notes - 5

    The Five Writing Superpowers - 6

Lesson One - Create a Pirate Character - 8

    Find Your Pirate Name - 9

Lesson Two - Create a Sensory Setting - 13

    Make a Pirate Poster - 15

Lesson Three - Create a Plot - 21

    Draw a Treasure Map - 25

    Play Hide the Treasure Map - 25

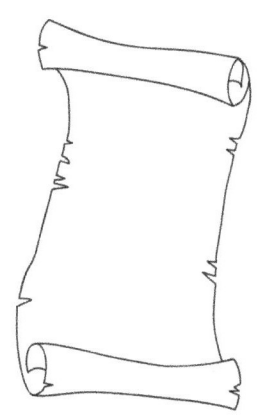

Lesson Four - Write the Beginning - 27

    How to Talk Like a Pirate - 29

    Make a Pirate Hat - 33

Lesson Five - Show, Don't Tell - 37

    Dress up and Talk Like a Pirate for a Day - 37

Lesson Six – Onomatopoeia - 42

    Make Your Own Pirate Code - 46

Lesson Seven - Write the Middle and Interjections - 50

    Interjections - 51

Lesson Eight - Strong Verbs – 56

    Using a Thesaurus – 56

    Illustrate a Scene from Your Story - 58

Lesson Nine – Dialogue – 61

    Make a Pirate Hook - 64

Lesson Ten – Spice Up Your Story with Adjectives - 67

    Make "Walk the Plank Jell-O Shark Cups" - 68

Lesson Eleven - End Your Story – 71

    Illustrate a Scene from Your Story - 71

Lesson Twelve – Edit and Put it All Together – 74

    Editing - 74

    Bake a "Pirate Map" Pizza - 75

    Pirate Flashlight Theater - 76

Title Page Cover Template - 79

Pirate Writing Paper - 82

About the Author - 93

Welcome to Yo, Ho, Ho!
Write a Pirate Adventure

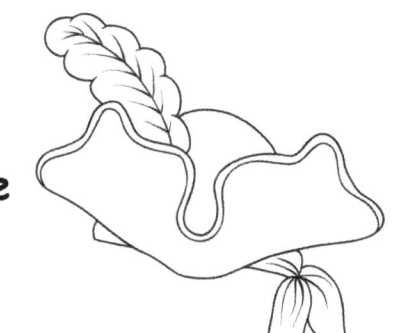

This is a fun and exciting creative writing curriculum designed to eliminate work for the teacher. This self-guided curriculum can be used in your homeschool, with multiple ages, or with a group.

I have taught creative writing for over fifteen years and have found that given the right tools, any child can write and love it. I encourage parents to use the *Five Writing Superpower* tools to create a writing adventure instead of a dull writing lesson. I have discovered in using these super powers that even the most reluctant writer will dive into the writing pool!

Creative Brainstorming - builds a bridge from brain to paper

Prewriting - sets up an irresistible story

Free Writing – writing without the fear of criticism unleashes the storyteller

Fun Thematic Activities – immerses the students in the writing theme thus creating an irresistible writing adventure

Gentle Grading - builds confidence, giving permission to be a child

The Five Writing Superpowers

Brainstorming - Never underestimate the creative power of brainstorming! Talking things out with your students helps to form ideas and primes the pump of creativity. Continue asking them about their characters and brainstorming ideas throughout the lessons. This also creates an excitement when they can share their ideas with you. This begins the writing adventure!

Prewriting - could be anything from writing down simple ideas to organizing thoughts on a list. Each prewriting activity helps the student formulate the story and organize their thoughts. It's like constructing a building in the students' mind so when it's time to put pencil on paper they have tons of ideas to draw from.

Free writing - is writing down whatever comes in a person's mind. Let your students write about what they love - zany plots, whacky characters, made up fantasy worlds and all. This will unleash the storyteller in your child and if they have been "stuck" it will open the flood gates for writing.

Theme immersion – Give your students fun activities that immerse them into the writing theme. This creates a rich atmosphere nourishing the imagination and creates a fun writing adventure.

Gentle grading - Don't make creative writing a lesson in grammar or spelling. Children will feel stifled if they must stop and sound out every word and fear that you will mark it wrong. Once they have a good start and feeling confident, begin correcting *gently*. This could easily be after a month or two. Introduce grammar rules in writing one at a time so they can build mastery before going on to a new rule.

This curriculum is user-friendly for grades 3-6 with easy, step-by-step instructions. Whether your student is a skilled writer or just starting out, this curriculum will inspire a love for writing. Fun activities and optional crafts in each lesson will keep your students happily busy for hours.

The course culminates at the end of twelve weeks with a story and a Flashlight Theater. This book teaches:

- Developing a character
- Using your senses in creating a setting
- How to spice up your dialogue
- How to create an interesting plot
- *Show, Don't Tell,* the golden rule of writing
- How to incorporate literary tools like onomatopoeia

There are twelve easy, self-guided lessons with 1-2 worksheets and an activity for each lesson. Each lesson is designed to last 45-60 minutes, which can be completed in one session or split up into two sessions. Each lesson has three components:

- Learning Time
- Writing Time
- Activity Time

Fun pirate crafts and foods throughout the book immerse the student in "pirate life," creating a springboard for telling a tall pirate tale. Find more pirate activities on my Pinterest page: https://www.pinterest.com/janmay2012/pirate-crafts/ Two great classic books to read alongside this lesson are *Swiss Family Robinson* and *Treasure Island.*

Lesson One – Create a Character

Lesson Time

The first thing to do in beginning a good story is to create an interesting character that you will enjoy reading about. A good character should have a few weaknesses to be realistic. If the character starts out selfish, give him opportunities to learn how to give. If he or she is fearful, give them a situation where they learn to face their fears and gain courage. If he struggles with shyness, give him a situation when he has to be outgoing or bold to save someone's life or keep someone safe.

Writing Time

Look at the code on the next page, "What's Your Pirate Name?" Using the code, figure out what your name is. Do this for your family's and friends' names too. Also think about names for your pirate captain and crew in your story.

Pirate Tidbit – A pirate ship could hold 15-125 crew members, depending on the size of the ship. That's a lot of men to feed and keep in order! There were several positions aboard a pirate ship. Below are a few of them:

Captain – head of the ship
Quartermaster – second in command when the captain was not around
Boatswain or the Bo'sun – supervised all activities on board the ship
Sailing master – in charge of navigation

Go on to the pages called "Create Pirate Characters" worksheets and fill them out.

Activity - What's Your Pirate Name?

Find the first letter of your first name. Then put in your real first name as a middle name. Use the sheet on the next page to write it down.

A – Awful	I – Black	R – Plunderin
B – Bowman	J – Jolly	S – Squidface
C – Captain	K – Long	T – Scurvy
D – Dirty	L – Landlubber	U – No good
E – Calico	M – Mama	V – Hurricane
F – First Mate	N – Swashbuckler	W – Salty
G – Greedy	O – Old	X – Bart
H – Quartermaster	P – Pegleg	Y – Atlantis
	Q – Grubby	Z – Dagger

Then find the first letter of your last name to find your pirate name.

A – Kidd	I – Bones	R – Cameroon
B – Sharkbait	J – Morgan	S – Poopdeck
C – Chumbucket	K – Codfish	T – Tuna Breath
D – Dreadful	L – Landlubber	U – Stinks-a-lot
E – Blackeye	M – Hook	V – McStubby
F – Bonne	N – Silver	W – Dirty Socks
G – McStinky	O – Old	X – Scallywag
H – Jones	P – Pegleg	Y – Longbeard
		Z – Scurvydog

Write the real name of the person on the left. Then use the code and write down their pirate name next to it.

Name _____ Pirate Name_____

Name _____ Pirate Name_____

Name _____ Pirate Name_____

Name _____ Pirate Name_____

Name _____ Pirate Name_____

Name _____ Pirate Name_____

Name _____ Pirate Name_____

Name _____ Pirate Name_____

Name _____ Pirate Name_____

Name _____ Pirate Name_____

Name _____ Pirate Name_____

Name _____ Pirate Name_____

Name _____ Pirate Name_____

Name _____ Pirate Name_____

Create Pirate Characters

Answer the questions for each of your characters below:

Pirate Character #1 Name _____

Age_____

Position in the ship's crew _____

Describe what he/she looks like:

_____

_____

Describe what she/he acts like: (funny, loud, energetic brave, hard worker, etc)

_____

_____

Pirate Character #2 Name _____

Age_____

Position in the ship's crew _____

Describe what he/she looks like:

_____

_____

Describe what she/he acts like: (funny, loud, energetic brave, hard worker, etc)

_____

_____

Pirate Character #3 Name
_____

Age_____

Position in the ship's crew _____

Describe what he/she looks like:
_____
_____

Describe what she/he acts like: (funny, loud, energetic brave, hard worker, etc)
_____
_____

Pirate Character #4 Name
_____

Age_____

Position in the ship's crew _____

Describe what he/she looks like:
_____
_____

Describe what she/he acts like: (funny, loud, energetic brave, hard worker, etc)
_____
_____

Lesson Two - Create a Setting

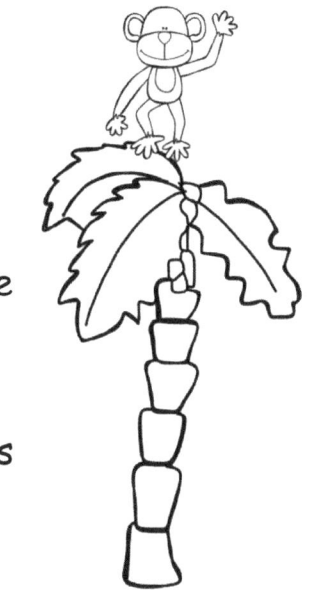

Lesson Time - A setting is the place and time in history where your story happens. Describing the setting for your story helps paint a backdrop for your characters, much like setting a stage for a play. For this story, the time in history would be during pirate days, which were from around 1500-1800AD. The place would be the ocean or seas and islands.

Make up a name for the island where your story takes place. Write it here: _____

Pre-Writing Time- On your island you can add ANY kind of animal or plants your mind can dream up! Are there Kanga-gators? Tiger-turtles? Flying Snakes? Create several new kinds of animals to use in your story. Write their names on the lines below (you can also write down regular animals).

_____   _____
_____   _____
_____   _____

On your island you can add ANY kind of plants, like rainbow trees, giant grass, or hamburger bushes. Make up several kinds of plants to include in your story, or you can write down regular plants.

_____   _____
_____   _____
_____   _____

You can even add a magic portal that takes your characters to a fantasy land like the wardrobe did in the book, *The Lion, the Witch, and the Wardrobe*. Your pirate characters can even time travel!

Create a Pirate Ship and Island Setting

Pre-Writing Time- It's important to describe the setting with vivid colors, sights, and sounds. Using all of your senses, make several lists below about the place your story happens.

Sights include colors:

Example: Turquoise Sea

_____
_____
_____
_____

Sounds include adjectives:

Example: Roaring Ocean

_____
_____
_____
_____

Smells include adjectives:

Example: Stinky Seaweed

_____
_____
_____
_____

Things with texture:

Example: Fuzzy Coconuts

_____
_____
_____
_____

Tastes include adjectives:

Example: Sweet Oranges

_____
_____
_____
_____

Activity – Make a Pirate Poster by coloring and cutting out the pictures on the next several pages and gluing them to a piece of poster board.

Lesson Three - Create a Plot

Lesson Time

A plot is a road map of what happens in a story scene by scene. It will guide you to write a good story. Organize your plot by filling in the answers to the questions below. This will help you figure out what will happen in your story.

A good story will increase the tension by *almost* letting the characters solve their problem, but they fail in the first attempt. The story becomes even more exciting if they fail twice.

Don't worry about writing the perfect idea. You can change anything later as you write the story. You might even think of a better idea along the way!

It's always more exciting if your pirate has to fight the sea dragon, weather a hurricane, or get swallowed by a whale. Let your imagination go wild and see how many things you can put in his way to stop him from finding the treasure. By the end of the story, however, let him find it. He might even get marooned on an island and have to build a tree house and hunt for food.

Pre-Writing Time – Fill out the worksheets on the next two pages by writing an outline for your story. It may not happen exactly the way you outline it. You might change it later and come up with a better idea.

Tell about the characters in your story. What is the first thing they do?

Write one - two sentences:
_____
_____
_____
_____
_____

What happens next? Write one - two sentences:
_____
_____
_____
_____

What happens next? Write one - two sentences:
_____
_____
_____
_____

What happens next? Write one - two sentences:
_____
_____
_____
_____

What happens next? Write one - two sentences:

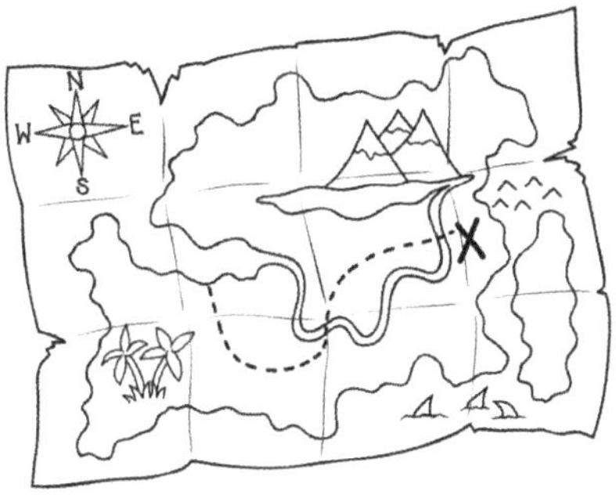

_____
_____
_____
_____

What happens next? Write one - two sentences:

_____
_____
_____
_____

What happens next? Write one - two sentences:

_____
_____
_____
_____

What happens at the end? Write one - two sentences:

_____
_____
_____
_____

Decorate the pirate below by adding a mustache or beard. Give him a sword or pistol, then give him a funny name. Draw a pirate ship or island behind him. Color the picture.

Activity - Draw a Treasure Map. Then cut it out, roll it up, and tie a string around it. Hide it somewhere in your house, room, or yard. Use a shoebox or plastic strawberry container for a treasure box. Add beads, fake coins, or jewelry. (Ask your mom for some!) Then hide it in a secret place. Have someone play along and search for the map and buried treasure. Draw trees, rivers, footprints, and an **X** for the buried treasure. Add how many steps or hops to each one. You can even leave a treat or treasure for them to find.

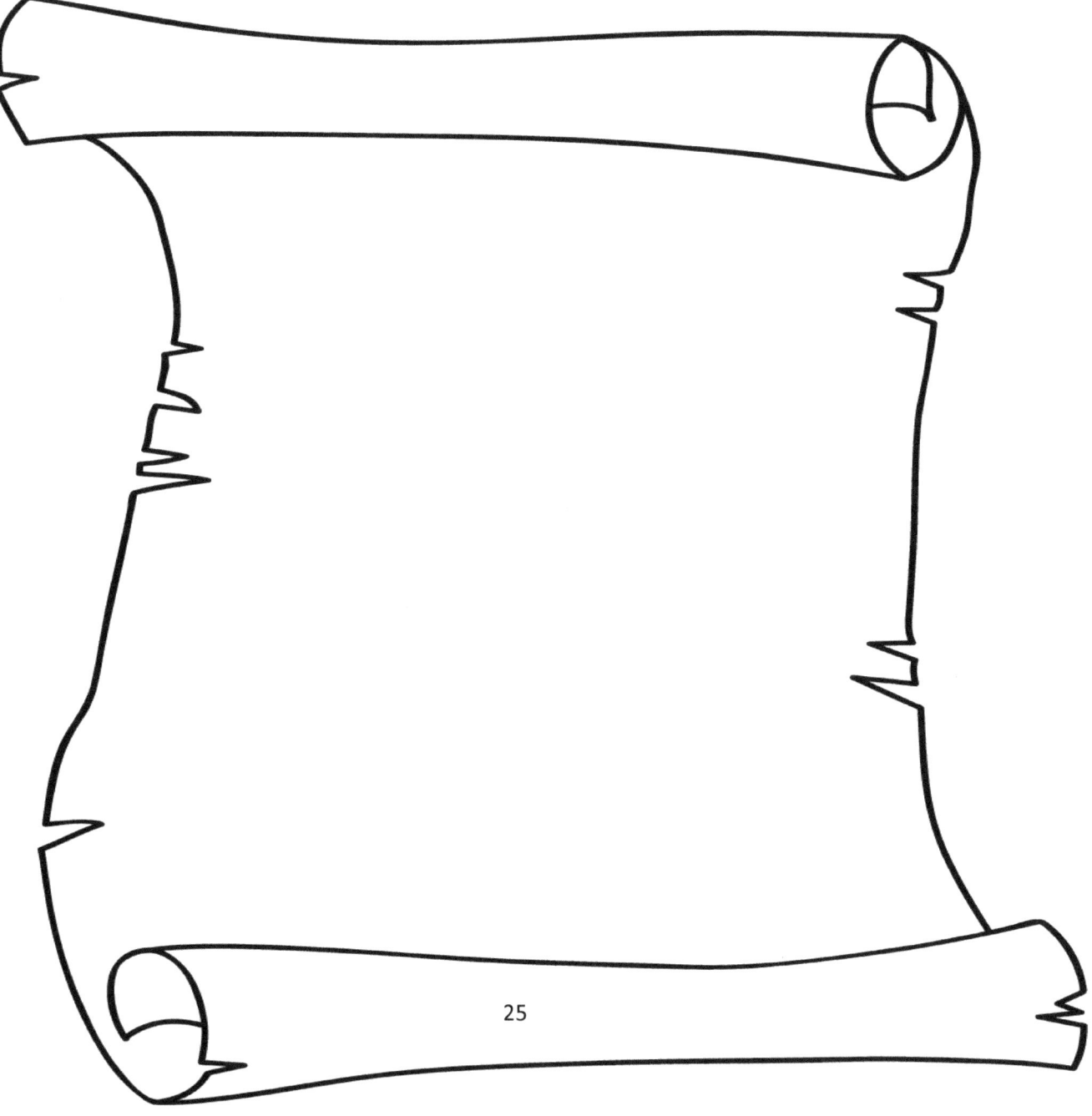

Lesson Four - Write the Beginning

Lesson Time

Every story has three major parts: a beginning, a middle, and an end.

The Beginning: The first sentences should start the story off right in the middle of interesting action to draw the reader in. This is called a HOOK. This should include your main character and the problem he or she faces.

The Middle of a story is where the character tries to solve the problem. It might even get worse. Think: drama, drama, drama! Some writers use the one, two, three method. The first two attempts to solve the problem fail and on the third try, the character succeeds.

The End is where the main characters overcome their problem. If it is a fable, they can grow in character in the process. If they start out fearful, they learn to be brave. If they start out selfish, they learn the joy of serving others.

Activity – Use Your Body Compass. Find out what direction the sun rises from your house. Stand, and with your body, let your right arm hang in that direction. That will always be east. Without moving, know that the other arm will always be west, where the sun sets. You are facing north and behind you is south. Whenever you are out in the wilderness, watch to see where the sun rises and you can do the same thing to find out which direction you are headed. This will help you find your way back to a safe zone if you get lost.

Write the Beginning of Your Pirate Adventure

Writing Time

Can you begin your story with interesting action? This is called a hook.

Write a HOOK for your story.

_____
_____
_____
_____
_____
_____
_____
_____

Every good story has a problem or two for the main character to solve. Write down several ideas to keep your pirates from finding the treasure too quickly:

_____
_____
_____
_____

Go on to the next page. Circle four "pirate talk" words to use in your story. Then go to the following pages and write a couple of paragraphs to begin writing your story.

Circle four "pirate talk" words or phrases below to use in your writing today. Then come back and use four more words each time you write.

Ahoy - Hello

Aye - yes

"Batten down the hatches!" – "Prepare the ship for a coming storm."

"Blimey!" - exhortation of surprise, shock, or disbelief

"Blow me down!" - expression of shock or disbelief. Much like "Oh, no!"

Booty – stolen pirate goods, money, jewelry, etc.

Buccaneer - a pirate

Bucko - a friend

Crow's Nest - small platform up high on the mast; used to spot ships from afar

Cutlass – favorite sword used by pirates, with a short, heavy, curved blade

Davy Jones' Locker - mythical place in the depths of the ocean where the evil Davy Jones takes sailors and pirates when they die

Doubloon – a gold Spanish coin found in pirates' stashes

"Heave Ho!" – "Work hard!"

Hornswaggle - to cheat someone out of something

Jolly Roger – the black pirate's flag with white skull and crossbones

Lily-livered – weak or cowardly

Landlubber – a person who doesn't know how to sail or is uncomfortable aboard a ship

Man-O-War – a pirate's ship ready for battle, with guns pointed out the sides and ready to fight.

Me - my

Old Salt - an experienced sailor

Pieces of Eight – Spanish silver dollars found in pirate stashes

Poop Deck – top deck on a large ship (*not* the bathroom)

Savvy? - Do you understand or agree?

Scallywag – an insult, saying one is an inexperienced pirate

Scurvy Dog - an insulting name

Seadog – a pirate who has a lot of experience

Shark Bait – If you walk the plank, the sharks will get you.

Shipshape - cleaned up and in order

"Shiver me timbers!" –"Oh, boy!"

Son of a Biscuit Eater - an insulting name

"Thar she blows!" – an expression when someone sees a whale

Walk the Plank – punishment where a person has to walk off a board hanging over the side of the ship while at sea. The person is taken to Davy Jones' Locker.

Ye - you

Yo-ho-ho - cheerful exhortation asking others to "Listen up!"

Begin writing your pirate story below. Skip a line as you write so it will be easier to edit later.

_____
_____
_____
_____
_____
_____
_____
_____
_____
_____
_____
_____
_____
_____
_____
_____
_____
_____
_____
_____
_____
_____
_____
_____

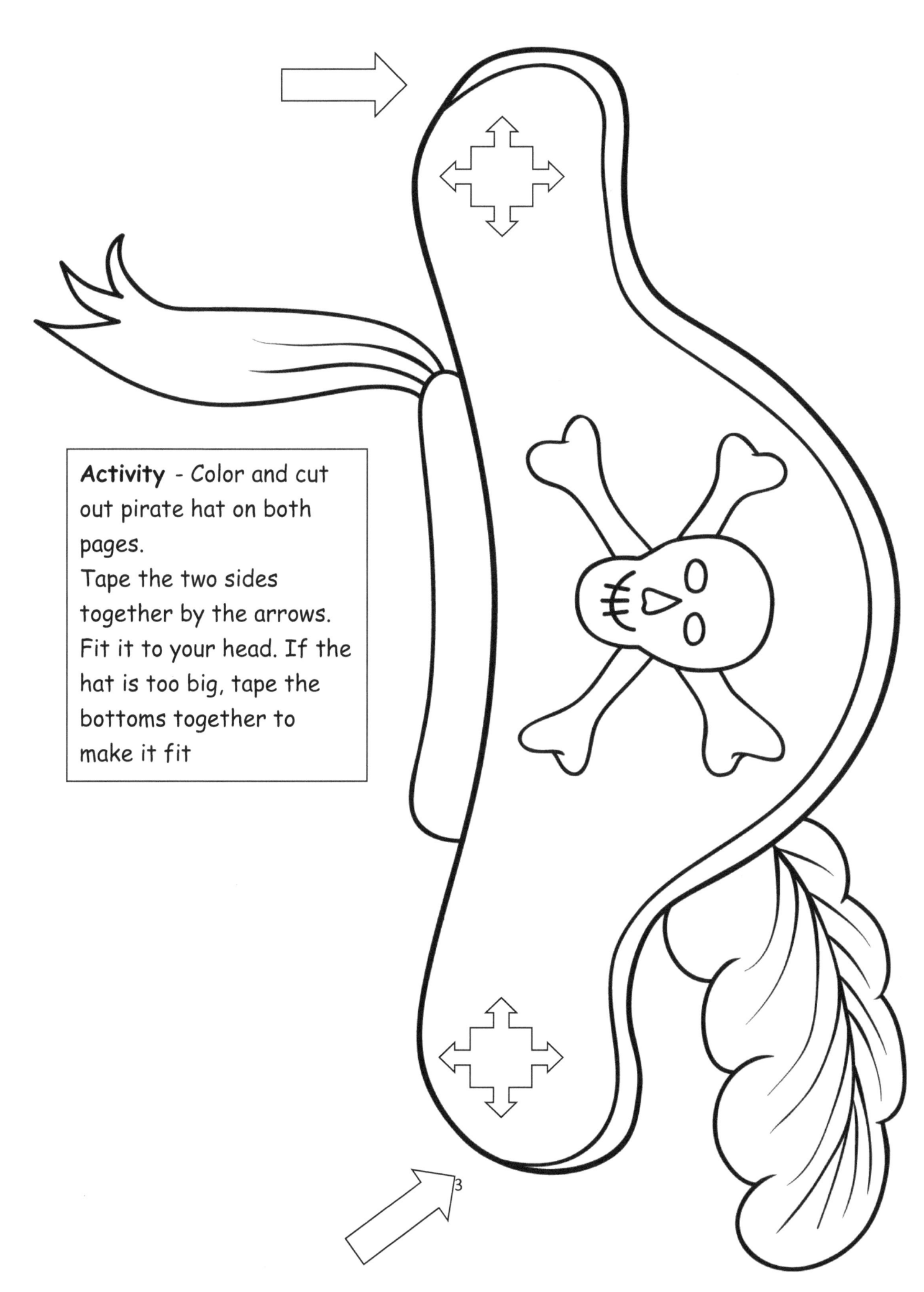

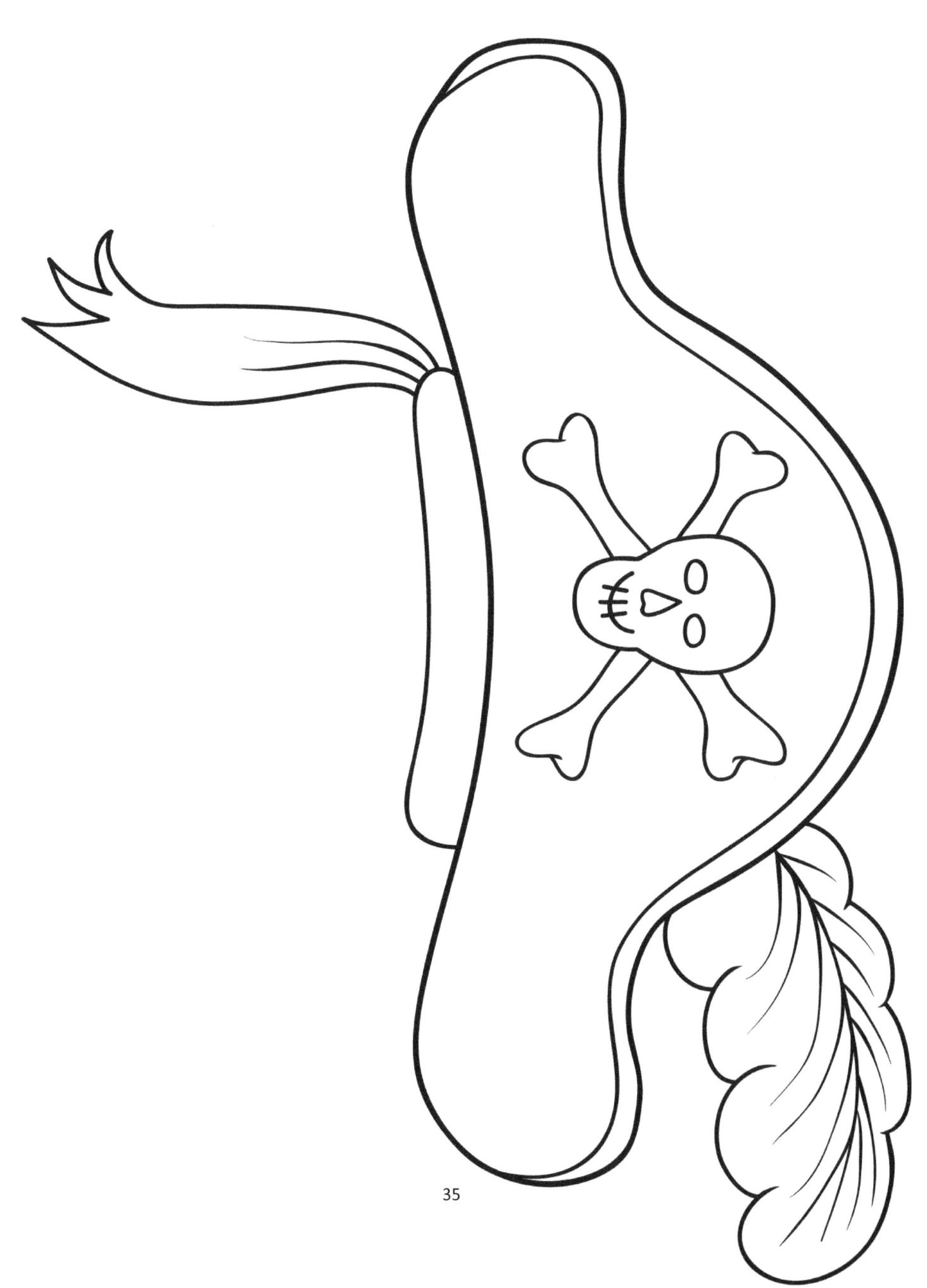

Lesson Five - "Show, Don't Tell"

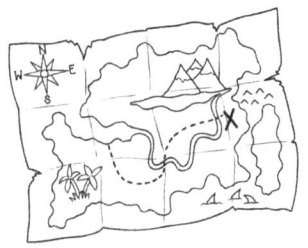

Lesson Time - C.S. Lewis, author of the popular Chronicles of Narnia series, once said, "Don't tell me that your character is afraid. Describe it in such a way that the very hairs on the back of my neck stand up when I read it." A good story describes the body language of the character's emotions, making the story come alive. This is the Golden Rule of Writing called "Show, Don't Tell."

Here are two examples of someone who is afraid:

1. Pete the pirate climbed the mast, when all of a sudden he heard a booming noise. He was afraid. **These sentences TELL the reader he is afraid.**

2. Pete the pirate sat in the tree, when all of a sudden he heard a booming noise. His heart pounded like a drum, and the hairs on the top of his head stood up. **These sentences SHOW the reader his body language when he was afraid.**

Activity- **Dress up and act and talk like a pirate for the day.** Turn an area of your house into a pirate ship. Make a tent on a pretend desert island and sleep there overnight. Cook pirate treasure map pizza for dinner (See page 75 for recipe). Invite your siblings or friends to join you. Make up pirate names and create a pirate hat or hook. Visit my Pinterest Pirate Craft Page for more ideas:
https://www.pinterest.com/janmay2012/pirate-crafts/

Practice the Golden Rule - "Show, Don't Tell"

Writing Time – Fill out the worksheets on the next two pages. Write several sentences showing how your character's body language changes with each new emotion.

Excitement

_____
_____
_____

Curiosity

_____
_____
_____

Anger

_____
_____
_____

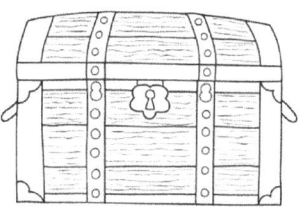

Fear

_____
_____
_____
_____

Pride

_____
_____
_____
_____

Happy

_____
_____
_____
_____

Continue writing your story on the next several pages.

Continue writing your pirate story below: Skip a line as you write so it will be easier to edit later.

_____
_____
_____
_____
_____
_____
_____
_____
_____
_____
_____
_____
_____
_____
_____
_____
_____
_____
_____
_____
_____
_____
_____
_____
_____
_____

Lesson Six - Onomatopoeia

Lesson Time - Onomatopoeia is when a word's pronunciation imitates its sound, like **swish**, **zoom**, and **zip**! These words can add fun sounds to your story! Read the list below out loud and see how they tickle your tongue.

When using these words as verbs, add "ing" or "ed" at the end: flipp<u>ed</u>, swish<u>ed</u>, slosh<u>ing</u>, whoosh<u>ing</u> etc.

OR use them as sounds by punctuating them with exclamation points. Example: Splash! Boom! Whoosh!

Circle the sounds below that make you think of sailing on pirate ship on an ocean.

Go on to the next two pages and fill out the worksheets.

Babble	Drip	Splish Splash
Bang	Drizzle	Splat
Bash	Fizz	Splash
Boink	Giggle	Sploosh
Bubble	Gurgle	Sprinkle
Clap	Hiss	Squirt
Clink	Kerplunk	Squish
Crash	Munch	Swish

Writing Time - Think of the characters in your story. Write a sentence for four of the onomatopoeia words that you circled on the previous page. Then draw a picture underneath it to illustrate your sentence.

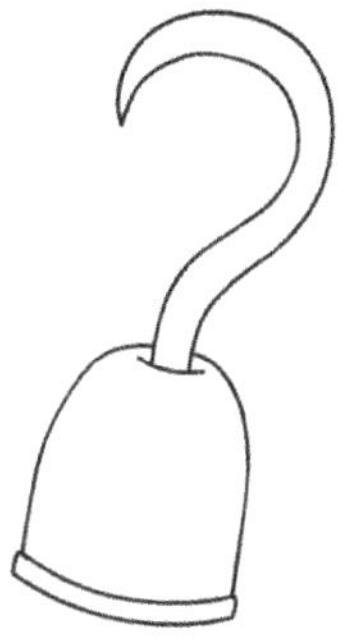

1. _____
   _____
   _____
   _____

2. _____
   _____
   _____
   _____

3.
_____
_____
_____
_____

4.
_____
_____
_____
_____

Pirate Tidbit - Even though pirates were scallywags when it came to obeying laws while fighting and pirating, they believed in law and order when aboard their own ship. Each pirate captain wrote a code that had to be followed . . . or else! When everyone does their own thing, it produces chaos, even on a pirate ship!

Here are a few points of the pirate code of a real pirate named Black Bart. He sailed in the early 1700s and captained the ship, *The Royal Fortune*. Modern language is used here so it is easier to understand. There were eleven points in Black Bart's Code, but below are only a few.

- Every man has an equal vote on what happens on the ship. Also, everyone has an equal share in food.

- Stealing is a crime – at least from another pirate aboard ship! (Most pirates made their living stealing from others but not from each other.) If you steal from another pirate, you shall have your nose and ears slit and be marooned (left alone) ashore on an island, where you shall be sure to encounter hardships.

- Stay battle-ready by keeping your weapons, cutlass, and pistols clean and ready for action at all times.

- Every man who is permanently injured during battle, like crippling, gets extra pay.

- The musicians shall rest on the Sabbath Day, and during any other times the crew says it's okay.

Activity – Make up your own pirate code on the next page.

This Here be the Pirate Code aboard the _____ ship. Under the Leadership of Captain_____

1. _____
   _____
   _____
   _____

2. _____
   _____
   _____

3. _____
   _____
   _____

4. _____
   _____
   _____

5. _____
   _____
   _____

6. _____
   _____
   _____

Pirate Tidbit -Musicians were in high demand on pirate ships because the life of a pirate sailing on a ship for days on end could be stressful and boring. The musicians would lead in sea shanties (songs) while the crew cleaned the deck, hoisted the sails, or practiced with their weapons. Music also was used in leading the pirates into battle, much like the drummer boys of the Revolutionary War. It gave the pirates courage to fight. Instruments played during the pirate era were fiddles, bagpipes, drums, or pennywhistles, but the most common musical instrument was a concertina, which was a smaller version of an accordion.

Take a listen to pirate music:
https://www.youtube.com/watch?v=pMKkX7ukvbc&list=PLDAFAr6LGkx1Mn6dAlDLORwLqo72qy5dL&index=4

Does your family have a list of rules everyone follows? If so, write them here:

_____   _____

_____   _____

_____   _____

_____   _____

_____   _____

_____   _____

Write several more paragraphs of your story today. Remember to skip a line.

Lesson Seven
Writing the Middle and Interjections

Lesson Time

The middle of a story is where the character tries to solve the problem. It's even more exciting if the problem gets worse. Think drama, drama, drama! Some writers use the one, two, three method. The first two attempts to solve the problem fail, but on the third try, the character succeeds. It's like a thrilling roller coaster ride! First you go up, then down and upside down, but finally you come back down to the ground.

Write 3 things in the circles below that can get in the way of the pirates from finding the treasure:

Go on to the next page.

An interjection is a part of speech that usually comes at the beginning of a sentence to show strong emotion, surprise, or excitement. They are usually punctuated with an exclamation point (or a comma if the feeling is not as strong).

The word in **bold** is the interjection in the examples below. Because some sentences are written in "pirate talk," the grammar is not correct.

Examples:

- **Hurray!** We found the buried treasure!
- **Blimey!** That be the biggest squid I ever saw!
- **Grrr!** He ate the last sardine.

Circle three interjections below that you would like to use in your story.

Ahoy	Aye-aye	Boo hoo
Blimey	Duh	Eek
Fiddlesticks	Hey, Hi, Hello	Hurray
Hmmm, Mmmm	Oh, Oh-Oh	Oh, dear
Okie-dokie	Ouch	Phew
Rats	Shhh	Tsk, tsk
Vroom	Yo,Ho,Ho	Whoa
Wow	Yahoo	Yo, ho, ho

Use interjections from the previous page and fill in the text boxes using the comic strip cartoons below.

Activity – Pirates had a lot of spare time while on board a pirate ship. When they weren't working or pirating, they played games like checkers, backgammon, cribbage, or card games. Pretend you are your character and play a game with your crew. Maybe a brother or sister could play along.

Write several more paragraphs of your story today. Remember to skip a line.

Lesson Eight - Strong Verbs

Lesson Time - All verbs show action, but all verbs are not the same in strength. "Wow words" are verbs that show a picture of what is going on and gives your story punch. Weak verbs are overused and wimpy. They don't show much of anything.

For example, you could say: "Captain Squidface ran across the sand."

The verb is <u>ran</u>. If he was in a hurry, you could say, he <u>darted</u> or <u>bolted</u> across the sand. These words add more punch.

A thesaurus is a helpful book of synonyms. It lists words that are similar to each other.

Using a thesaurus, look up each word below and write two stronger ways to write each verb.

Fall   _____   _____

Walk   _____   _____

Carry   _____   _____

Limp   _____   _____

Crawl   _____   _____

Stronger Ways to Say "Went"

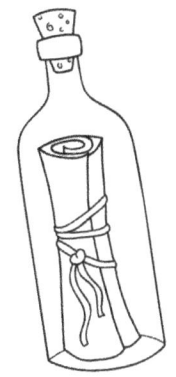

Writing Time - The word **went** is a weak verb. Try to use it as little as possible. Below are words to use instead of went. **Circle ten words** from this list and see if you can change any "went" uses in your story and replace them with the circled words. Then continue writing your story on the next pages.

Advanced	Fell	Rambled
Ambled	Flew	Retreated
Approached	Flitted	Roamed
Ascended	Floated	Rocketed
Barreled	Followed	Rushed
Blasted	Glided	Sailed
Bolted	Groveled	Scrambled
Boogied	Hastened	Scuttled
Bounced	Hightailed	Slithered
Bounded	Hiked	Staggered
Burst	Hoofed it	Stormed
Chugged	Hopped	Stumbled
Climbed	Hurdled	Traipsed
Crawled	Hurried	Vanished
Crept	Inched	Ventured
Cruised	Journeyed	Waddled
Danced	Loped	Wafted
Darted	Marched	Whisked
Dashed	Nosed	Withdrew
Encroached	Pounced	Wormed
Entered	Pushed on	Zipped

Activity - Draw a picture of what is happening in your story below. Color it and save it in a folder to add to this pirate story when you put it all together at the end.

Write several more paragraphs of your story today. Remember to skip a line.

Lesson Nine - Dialogue

Lesson Time: Dialogue is when a person in your story is talking. Good dialogue adds interest and action to any story. Use quotation marks at the beginning, when your characters first start to talk, and again at the end when they are finished. Put all ending punctuation marks (like periods, question marks, or exclamation marks) *inside* the quotation marks.

Example:

"Hoist the sales and chase that ship," said the Quartermaster.

There are two parts to a sentence of dialogue. The first part is the quote; the second part is the dialogue tag. You separate them with a comma, unless you use an exclamation or question mark.

Example:

"Hoist the sales and chase that ship," is the quotation.

"Said the Quartermaster" is the dialogue tag.

There are many different ways to say "said" that can bring your story to life.

Example: Instead of using "said" in the above example you can say:

"Hoist the sales and chase that ship!" shouted the Quartermaster.

This paints a vivid picture much better than just using "said." You can pepper fun dialogue tags throughout your story. **Go on to the next page.**

Stronger Ways to Say "Said" in a Dialogue Tag

admitted
agreed
answered
argued
asked
barked
begged
boasted
boomed
bragged
bellowed
blurted
complained
confessed
cried
defended
declared
demanded
denied
exclaimed
giggled
hesitated
hissed
hinted
hollered
howled
interrupted
joked
laughed
mumbled

muttered
nagged
objected
ordered
pleaded
promised
proclaimed
questioned
recalled
remembered
roared
scolded
scoffed
screamed
snarled
snorted
soothed
squawked
stammered
suggested
taunted
tattled
teased
whimpered
whooped
whispered
yapped
yakked
yelled
yelped

Circle 10 words to use in your story.

Writing Time - Write a line of dialogue in each text box. Add quotation marks and a fun dialogue tag from the words you circled on the previous page.

Activity - Make a Pirate Hook for your Hand

- Ask for your parents' help to poke a little slit in the bottom of a red or blue plastic cup. The end of a sharp scissors works well for this. Make sure the slit isn't too big, so the pipe cleaner doesn't wiggle around and fits securely.

- Thread a silver pipe cleaner through the hole and tie a knot on the other side of the cup.

- Shape the other end of the pipe cleaner into a hook.

- Make your hand into a fist and stick it in the cup.

- Have fun being Captain Hook!

Pirate Tidbit – Pirates sailed across deep oceans and saw many great sea animals along the way. Some must have looked like monsters, including giant squid with long tentacles that could have been forty feet long. Pirates might have seen sperm whales, sharks, and other deep-sea creatures. There were also legends of a scary sea monster called the Kraken, which was probably a giant squid. It was said to have wrapped its long tentacles around ships to sink them and take its prey down to Davey Jones' locker. Maybe your pirates fight a battle with the Kraken!

Write several more paragraphs of your story today. Remember to skip a line and add some fun dialogue tags.

Lesson Ten
Spice Up Your Story with Adjectives

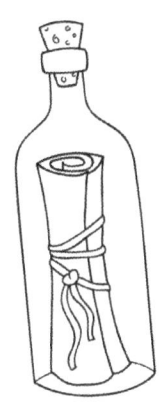

Lesson Time

An adjective is a describing word that helps nouns by telling "which one," "what kind," "how much," etc. Add an adjective in each of the blanks below for practice:

1. The _____ pirate climbed the _____ pole and hoisted the Jolly Roger.

2. The _____ island was covered with _____ trees.

3. The _____ captain shouted, "Clean that _____ poopdeck!"

4. The only food the pirates had for days was some _____ bread and _____ oranges.

5. A giant _____ sea monster wrapped it's _____ tentacles around the _____ ship.

6. The two _____ pirates swung their _____ swords in the air.

7. The _____ sails floated in the wind until a _____ storm overtook the ship.

67

Writing Time

A noun is a person, place, or thing. An adjective is a word that describes nouns like "how big," "what color," "how much," etc. Go to page 1 of your story and circle the nouns. Add an adjective above each one. Then continue writing another couple of paragraphs of your story.

Activity - Teddy Graham Pirates Walking the Plank

- 1 large box of blue Jell-O
- 6 small 6-oz plastic cups
- Teddy bear shaped crackers
- ½ gram cracker for each cup as a plank
- 6-12 gummy sharks
- black decorator icing in tube for hats and eye patches
- 4 Tbsp. cake frosting any flavor

Instructions:

- Make Jell-O as instructed on the box.
- Place 6 plastic cups in a larger plastic container for easy transport to freezer.
- Ladle the Jell-O into the plastic cups and place in freezer.
- After 20 minutes, add gummy sharks to Jell-O and put in **refrigerator** until the Jell-O is set completely
- While you are waiting, you can break the gram crackers into single pieces to place across the cup as planks.
- Use colored decorator's frosting in the tube to apply hats and eye patches to teddy gram bears. Use a little dollop of frosting to help him stand on the plank.

Write several more paragraphs of your story today. Remember to skip a line.

Lesson Eleven - End your Story

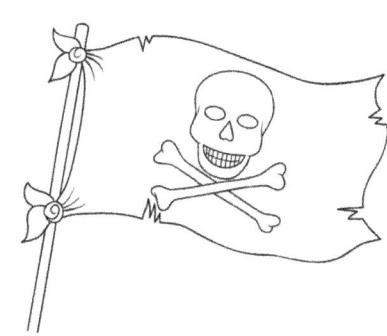

Lesson Time

Ending a story is helping the characters find the treasure. If you want your character to learn a good life lesson, then it's also time to give them an "ah-ha" moment, where they realize they have learned something.

Writing Time – On the next several pages, finish your story. If you need more paper, go to the back of the book for extra pages.

Activity – **On a piece of white paper** draw and color a scene from your story. Save it in a folder so you can add it to your story when you put all the pages together to make a book.

Continue and finish your story here. Remember to skip a line. More pages are in the back of the book if you need them.

Lesson Twelve - Editing and Putting It All Together

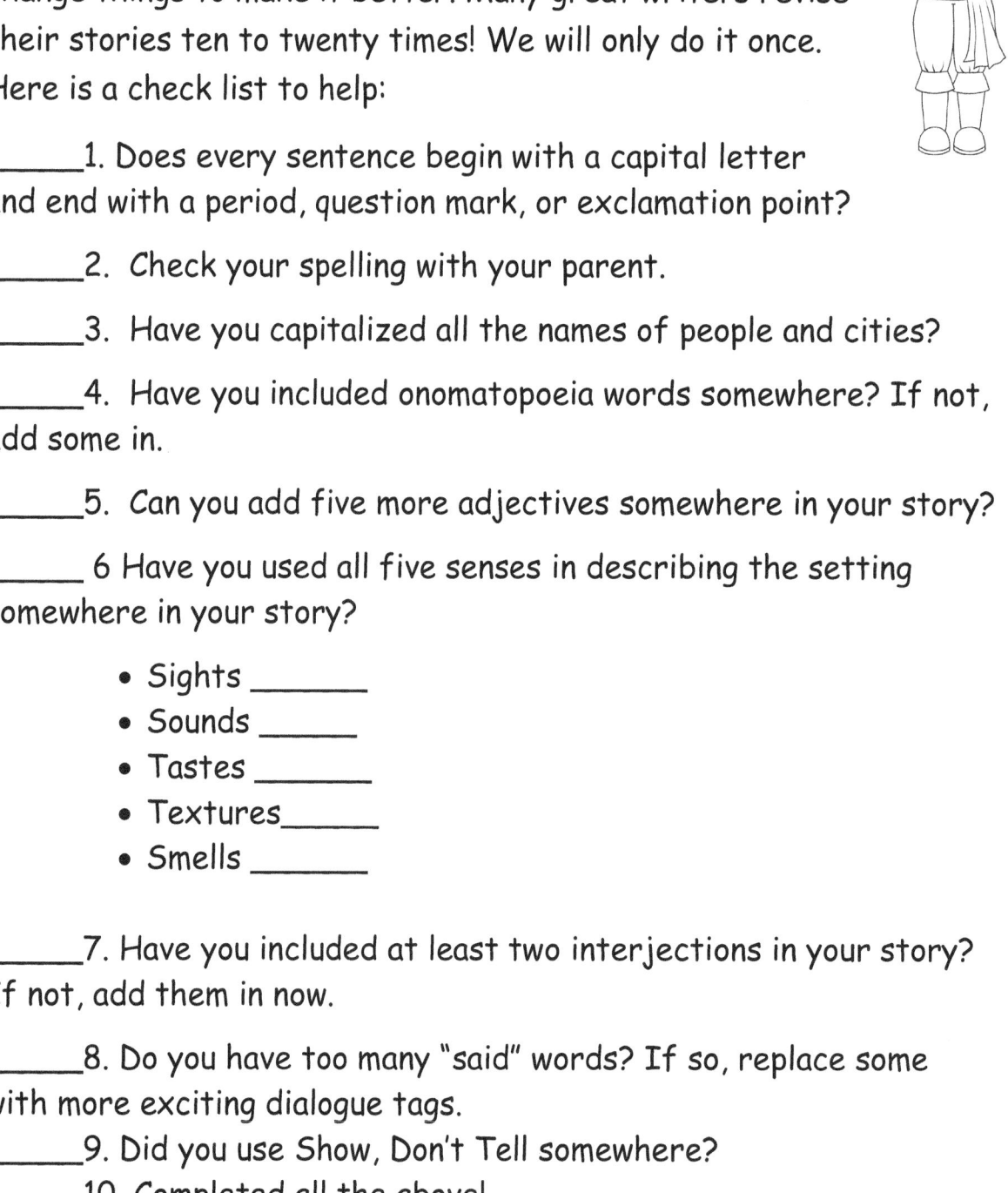

Lesson Time: To edit means to correct any errors and change things to make it better. Many great writers revise their stories ten to twenty times! We will only do it once. Here is a check list to help:

_____1. Does every sentence begin with a capital letter and end with a period, question mark, or exclamation point?

_____2. Check your spelling with your parent.

_____3. Have you capitalized all the names of people and cities?

_____4. Have you included onomatopoeia words somewhere? If not, add some in.

_____5. Can you add five more adjectives somewhere in your story?

_____ 6 Have you used all five senses in describing the setting somewhere in your story?

- Sights _____
- Sounds _____
- Tastes _____
- Textures_____
- Smells _____

_____7. Have you included at least two interjections in your story? If not, add them in now.

_____8. Do you have too many "said" words? If so, replace some with more exciting dialogue tags.

_____9. Did you use Show, Don't Tell somewhere?

_____10. Completed all the above!

Activity - Bake a Treasure Map Pizza

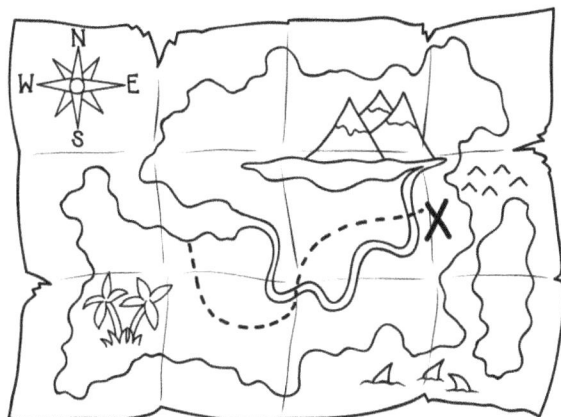

- Store bought pizza dough – shape into an oblong for a map affect. Follow directions on the package.

- Jar of pizza sauce – spoon even layer on top of dough

- 1-2cups shredded mozzarella cheese – sprinkle over top

- Black olive halves or black beans for footprints

- Parsley or mushroom slices for trees

- Green pepper boats – Use a curvy slice for the bottom. Cut out squares and triangles for sails. Using a toothpick, poke a square and triangle for the sails and flag.

- Pepperoni cut into triangles for mountains and squares for houses

- Red pepper slices – lay 2 slices over each other to make an X to mark where the buried treasure is. Be creative and add your own ideas too. Don't bake the boats!

- Bake according to package. Don't forget to take a photo.

Putting It All Together

Fill out and color one of the title pages on the next several pages.

Neatly rewrite your story on notebook paper or gently, pull out all your final story pages, maps, and drawings throughout the book. Number them and trim the edges. Arrange them by putting all drawings and maps in the right places. Three-hole punch all the pages then put them into a plastic essay binder along with your title page. The essay binders can be found at a superstore or office supply store.

Activity - Host a Yo, Ho, Ho Pirate Party and Flashlight Theater

Host a pirate party and flashlight theater. Students can make a theater box by cutting out a large square in a big box. Paint it black, and then read behind it after it's dry. Students can also choose to read at a table, on a living room chair, or in a tent with a flashlight shining on their story. When the audience arrives, turn all the lights out in that room and flash several flashlights on the reader as your student reads their stories. They may also act out the story like a play in pirate days using props like hooks and swords. Remember to follow good flashlight behavior: No flashing in anyone's eyes or waving lights around to make fun patterns on the wall. This will distract the reader! Invite grandparents, friends, cousins, or other families to share in your pirate party to be in the audience or read their own stories. Make fun pirate food to share! ☺

Make your own Sea Dog Snack Mix for Pirate Flashlight Theater

  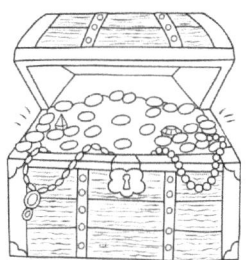

Set out 10 different snack items in bowels with spoons. Let each person add a scoop of their favorite snack into a plastic sandwich bag and shake them together!

Salty Snacks

- Small cheese fish crackers
- Cheese or plain popcorn
- Pretzels, plain, or chocolate covered
- Corn chips
- Cooked bacon pieces
- Nuts – watch for allergies!
- Tiny peanut butter or cheese-filled crackers
- Sunflower seeds

Sweet Snacks
- Chocolate chips
- Butterscotch chips
- Brownie or cookie pieces
- Gummy sharks
- Caramel popcorn
- Marshmallows
- Raisins
- Dried fruits - apricots or cherries cut up

Decorate the pirate below by adding an eye patch, mustache, or beard. Give him a sword or pistol then give him a funny name. Draw a pirate ship or island behind him, then color the picture.

 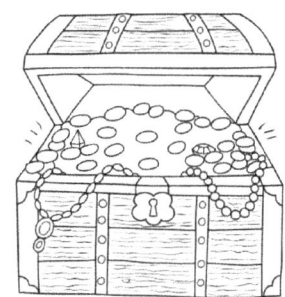 

_____

BY

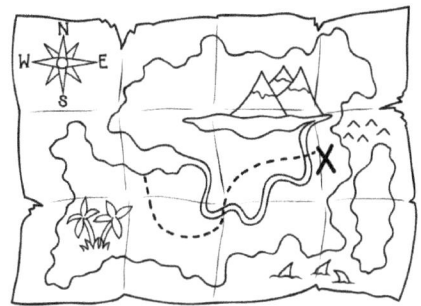

_____

BY

_____

Extra Pages

Creative Writing Made Easy . . . Helping Every Child Succeed

About the Author

Jan May loved homeschooling her two children through high school. Whether it was attending re-enactments of the Revolutionary War or collecting an amphibian zoo, hands-on education was always at the forefront of her curriculum.

She is author of the *Creative Writing Made Easy* series that engages even the most reluctant writers with the Five Writing Super Power approach. All of the books are filled with fun interactive language activities involving each type of learner: visual, auditory, and kinesthetic-perfect for the wiggle in boys. Having been a creative writing teacher for over fifteen years, she believes that given the right tools, every child can learn to write and love it!

Visit her website for fun downloads and activities. Watch for her online teaching schedule- leading students and teens in a fun and engaging writing experience!

If you like this book, you might also enjoy

Knights and Castles Writing Adventure
Spies of the Revolutionary War Writing Unit
Battle Cry! Write a Soldier's Adventure

Order this book and more at www.NewMillenniumGirlBooks.com and wherever homeschool books are sold.

www.ingramcontent.com/pod-product-compliance
Lightning Source LLC
Chambersburg PA
CBHW061113070526
44583CB00027B/3274

9 781732 111929